App Inventor 2 with MySQL database
remote management of data

by
Antonio Taccetti

Inspirational phrases

Within the confines of your computer, you are the creator.
Controls, at least potentially, anything that happens to you.
If you're good enough, you can be a God.
On a small scale.
Linus Torvalds

Computers are incredibly fast, accurate and stupid.
Humans are incredibly slow, inaccurate and brilliant.
Jointly constitutes an incalculable force.
Albert Einstein

Table of contents

Contents of this guide

This guide explains how to use App Inventor 2 to create an App for Android OS that interfaces with tables in MySQL database.

From your Android device you'll can:

- Order any field in the table in ascending and descending order
- Filter the data in a field of your choice, even the same order.
- Import the Android device database records.
- Share (Sharing) these records showing a list of App installed on your device, including those that can handle the information provided, allowing the user to choose which of these should be used.
  - For example App for emails, social networking, messages and so on. -

To create the MySQL database and the php part is explained:

- How to get software for free to install an Apache development environment with local server php / MySQL.
- Described the phpMyAdmin software component showing how to create and test tables for local and remote even with the use of query
- Shown how to write a php page that allows you to enter, edit and delete data and records from tables in a database.
- How to design and write the php web page that allows Android App to interface with the MySQL database table allowing you to:
  - Sort and filter the data contained in the tables of a database on the Internet
  - Transfer on the Android device record
- How to manage more options about obtaining an Internet server at low cost or free of charge.
  - Displayed or how to load php interface and chart php / MySQL on the Internet by testing the operation server.

App for Android, php pages and tables could be downloaded from author's website. Links are listed at the end of this guide.

These are:

1. App_Web_PHP_MySQL: App zipped file containing the threshing floor and the APK
2. ai2tabella: Table Database
3. ai2-connessionedb.php and ai2connessionedb.php: Database connection.
4. ai2-index.php and ai2index.php: Access the administration page of the database
5. ai2-accessosessione.php ai2accessosessione.php: Verify the database access data

6.   ai2-gestionedati.php and ai2gestionedati.php: Entering, editing data
7.   ai2-interfaccia.php and ai2interfaccia.php: Interface page with the Android APP

These php pages are written for two different language's versions:
those with the hyphen - in the name are for the older one.

Eg:

- Ai2-connessionedb.php: older version of php
- Ai2connessionedb.php: Recent php version (5.5 years in 2016)

For those interested in using the library of graphical php (GD library), expanding and enriching the interface between APP Android and php / MySQL, in bookstores on the Internet can be found in the help:
Use GD library with php: functions, figures, graphics and gradients.
In Italian, it contains detailed examples on how to create charts and graphs without the use of additional libraries.

Furthermore in support of the guide, at this web address:
http://www.taccetti.net/web/phpgd2/index.php?id=117

php pages shows how to create dynamic graphics with this language.

database

In computer language, the English word database (in Italian, database) defines data archives structured in order to streamline the management and updating of information, supporting the conduct of complex investigations.

The information contained in the databases are structured and linked together according to valued logic models and chosen by designers.

The simplest database is a table comparable to a squared paper.

This table contains data related to a specific topic, such as a table of Italian regions, or customers or products, classic examples are the phone books but also an Excel spreadsheet from Microsoft or OpenOffice Calc.

In this spreadsheet / chart, each line corresponds to an item and stored in the database and is technically called a record or tuple.

Each record in a table contains informations of one (and only one) particular item.

For each item is intended, an individual, a commodity, an event etc.

The records, in turn, are divided and are constituted by parts which together, are the attributes of the record as a whole.
These parts are called fields.

The fields are presented in the columns of squared paper mentioned earlier.
For example, fields for human beings could be: name, surname, date of birth, address etc.
for an item: unit cost, provenance, weight etc.

With reference to Excel and Calc software already mentioned, the columns represent the fields and rows records.

In practice, referring to the table of the Italian regions, each record could describe a region and every field intended to contain, name of the region, notes, surface area in square kilometers, date and time of the last updating records etc.

A table name "ai2tabella" containing the Italian regions could be so represented:

id	nome	note	data
1	Toscana	Abitanti 3692433, situata nell'Italia centrale, con capoluogo Firenze.	2016-04-11 12:28:15
2	Umbria	Regione dell'Italia centrale di 889497 abitanti posta nel cuore della penisola.	2014-03-19 14:18:10
3	Lazio	Abitanti 5566783 abitanti, con capoluogo Roma che è anche capitale d'Italia.	2012-09-13 21:23:40

In the above table "ai2tabella", the elements of a record, the fields, are identified by a name.

In addition, there is a field called id, it is the index field.
Although the indexes are optional, their can make much faster sorting and searching operations, especially on large amounts of data.

Within the same database, the name of each table must be unique.
The same field name may instead be used in different tables of the same database.

But whereas research in the database are then performed by invoking names of tables and fields, best avoided, as often as possible, the duplication of names of the columns (fields).
It will be thus avoided complicating the project and subsequent data search.

Every field, so each column of the table, can contain different data types (field properties), integers, floating point, alphabetic characters (technically referred to as strings) etc.

To summarize:

- The amount of records is virtually infinite, being its limit the amount of space of the media that contains them.
- The amount of the fields and the type of data that each of them can contain is defined by those who design the database.

The purpose of a database is to convert data into information.
If we consider the information as knowledge, the two terms are not interchangeable, indeed, there is much difference between them.

- Data is a collection of facts.
- Information is data organized or presented in an appropriate way to make decisions.

DataBase Managment Systems

There are many DBMS (DataBase Managment Systems) which are software that implements the functions to use the database.
These functions are: data access, updating, research and selection (also called filtering), the latter in a manner that can be chosen by users, etc.
The best known software of these DBMSs are: MySQL, Oracle, MS SQL, PosgreSQL, etc.

scalability

Often reads "database scalability", which is the ability to maintain the integrity of the performance of the database with increasing amount of data, the queries performed and, even more important, as it is possible to expand the design of the database by adding tables, fields and functionality.

php

PHP (recursive acronym for "PHP: Hypertext Preprocessor" Hypertext Preprocessor, is an interpreted scripting language, originally designed for programming dynamic web pages. The php interpreter is a free software distributed under the PHP License.
It supports all DBMS more 'widespread.

MySQL types of tables

The tables used by MySQL are varied, the main ones are

MyISAM

Type defined by default, it ensures excellent performance in speed in data search

InnoDB

More comprehensive than MyISAM, but slower because of the additional features available to them.
Today (2016) to increase the power of the machine, the performance difference between MyISAM and InnoDB has become minimal.

This type of tables are not always available in the hosting cost.

SQL

SQL (Short Query Language) is the language used for operations in DBMS.
Despite being available in many dialects, these are very similar to each other even if implemented on very different systems.
To define actions to be performed on the data and databases, SQL uses an almost natural syntax.

The commands are in English and the words / commands identify the function they perform (select to select, delete to delete, update to upgrade and so on).
Everything is in assimilating the way in which the phrase is composed / SQL command and the rest "comes from itself."

Query

The user use this term to specify the query in a database (select, insert, delete, update etc.).

Queries use SQL language (Structured Query Language).
The analysis of the result of the query is the subject of relational algebra study.

Queries are commonly used in php pages or similar language and are divided into two types:

- Request information, such as data selection queries
  - SELECT: used to select data from tables

- Editing commands, such as deletion, insertion or correction
  - INSERT: insert data into tables
  - UPDATE: modify data in tables
  - DELETE: delete data from tables
- Among the action queries are also covered
  - CREATE: create tables
  - ALTER: modify the table structure
  - DROP: drop the tables

The latter group commands are usually used in the creation of the database, and much less in normal daily use.

php/MySQL tools

Database development spaces

There are several software that autonomously create the development spaces and allow you to start quickly with the implementation of projects, EasyPHP, LAMP (Linux Apache MySQL PHP) or WAMP (Windows Apache MySQL PHP), in continuation we refer to XAMPP.

XAMPP is multi-platform, which means that it works on Linux, Mac and Windows environments.
On the website https://www.apachefriends.org/it/index.html are available and downloadable packages for different Operating Systems and in various languages.
XAMPP is a simple and light Apache distribution, it makes it extremely simple to beginners and developers create web server on your local PC.
The software is designed for easy installation and an intuitive use.

In XAMPP includes a web application server (Apache), a DBMS (MySQL), and a scripting language (php).
The supplied software is free and reproduction is free.
Very important is the fact that many of the Internet server environments using the same components, this makes it simple and intuitive to copy php tables and pages from a local system to a web server on the Internet.

web server

Software, running on a server, that can manage requests to transfer client's web pages, typically a web browser.
The set of the whole interconnected web server gives life to the World Wide Web.

A web server installed on the local PC simulates the behavior that you would have on Intenet, allowing more convenience test, thus facilitating corrections.

XAMPP, main components

- Apache: most popular web server in the world, processes and responds to requests by returning the content to the client computer (the applicant)
- MySQL: Described above, Open Source and free.
  It is used, among others, by Joomla and WordPress, allows the realization professional applications.
- Php: As described above, with it working Joomla, Drupal and WordPress. Trusted by thousands of developers, simple to learn, he works perfectly with MySQL.
- Perl is a powerful programming language, feature-rich, with over 25 years of development.
- PhpMyAdmin, written in php, is a free software, distributed under the GNU license.
  It allows you to administer the database, create tables, queries, etc. tested.
  The latest version can also be downloaded from the official website
  http://www.phpMyAdmin.net/

INSTALL XAMPP

Despite the simplicity and the quality of the package, someone may find some difficulties. Some attention can be:

- Temporarily Disable the anti-virus before installation.
- Install the package making you click the right button> Run as administrator.

In one screen, usually the second, you can choose which components to install.
For simplicity, or not knowing what exactly to do, leave everything as default.
If necessary, uncheck 'Learn more about BitNami for XAMPP'

The XAMPP installation can take several minutes, the time may also depends on the performance of the PC in use.
Once installed will be available a control panel from which you can check and set all the XAMPP components and start or stop the services.

At the end of the installation the software should be located in the folder C: \ xampp \
Obviously the letter C can be different if you chose to install on another disk.

XAMPP, installation verification

Once downloaded and installed XAMPP must check its success.

Go to C:\xampp (or adequate lettre) and double click on the file xampp_start.exe
It should see the XAMPP Control Panel

Launch any browser and in the address bar write:
http: // localhost /

You should see the main page of XAMPP with the title:
XAMPP Apache + MySQL + PHP + Perl

In the latest versions instead of XAMPP Apache + MySQL + PHP + Perl might look:
XAMPP + Apache + PHP + Perl MariaDB

On the mariadb website
https://mariadb.com/kb/it/mariadb-vs-mysql-compatibilita/
The English-language pages are at: https://mariadb.com/

you can read:
For all practical purposes, MariaDB is a binary replacement for MySQL, ready to use, which can replace the corresponding version (eg MySQL 5.1 -> 5.1 MariaDB, MySQL 5.2 -> 5.2 MariaDB, MySQL 5.3 -> 5.3 MariaDB) .

Here's what it means:

The data and the table definition file (.frm) are binary compatible.

All client APIs, protocols and structures are identical.
All file names, the tracks, paths, ports, sockets, etc should be equal.
All MySQL connectors (PHP, Perl, Python, Java, .NET, MyODBC, Ruby, MySQL C connector etc) behave the same way with MariaDB.

There are some installation problems with php5 of which is better to be aware (it is a bug in the way the old controls the php5 client library compatibility).
The mysql-client package also works with MariaDB server.
This means that in most cases simply uninstall MySQL and install MariaDB to use it.
There is no need to convert the data files if you are using the same version, such as 5.1.

Check at the same site, for updates.

If XAMPP does not start its components, one of the most frequent problems is the use of port 80 that XAMPP uses by default while the same port is also used by Skype and Windows 10.

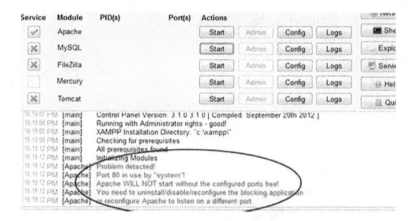

In the case of Skype, just do not use it in conjunction with XAMPP.
If Skype is launched after XAMPP, usually Skype starts listening on a different port and everything runs smoothly.

In the case of Windows 10, but also for Skype that relocate it to listen on a different port it may be desirable to change the listening port for XAMPP varying it by 80 to another.
To this address
http://pepfry.com/tutorials/solve-issue-port-80-in-use-by-system-xampp
you can read a thorough tutorial.
However, this is to change the contents of httpd.conf,
to do it:

- Go to the C: \ xampp \ apache \ conf
- Make a copy of httpd.conf to be kept ready to replace the original in case of errors.
- Open the httpd.conf file with the Windows Notepad
- Modifier voice Listen 80 to Listen 81 (or other number)
- Restart all
- Launch a browser and in the address bar, type http: // localhost: 81 / and everything should be okay.

Solutions for other inconvenineti indeed very rare, can be read at:

http://www.corsijoomla.com/xampp-non-parte-apache-mysql.html

XAMPP, the Control Panel

To start the XAMPP control panel, you have to go to C: \ xampp (or appropriate drive letter), and double-click on the file xampp_start.exe

The XAMPP control panel gives you complete control of all the components installed with XAMPP.
You can use the panel to start / stop several modules, starting the Unix shell, open Windows Explorer to view all running background tasks.

Here's a quick overview of the control panel.

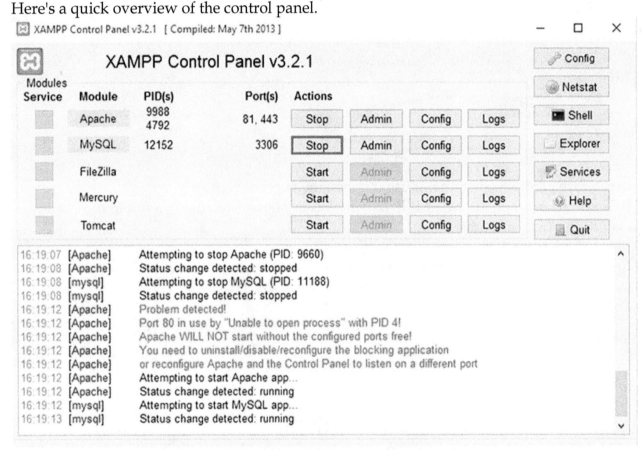

Apache's services are running on port 81 and MySQL

To make it more in line with the habits of xampp_start.exe icon can be inserted in the Windows Start menu in the Windows taskbar, (click on the icon with the right mouse button and choose item from the menu which opens)
To stop everything just click on the Stop button in the Control Panel.

php test

Once everything looks good the last test is to try php.
During the installation of XAMPP it should be created phpinfo.php the files within the folder C: \ xampp \ htdocs \ dashboard \ or C: \ xampp \ htdocs \

The local server can be configured in many ways, but it is beyond the scope of this guide.

Launch a browser and in the address bar, type the address of phpinfo.php files, for example:

http: //localhost/dashboard/phpinfo.php

or

http: // localhost: 81 / dashboard / phpinfo.php

If the port number has been changed.

The phpinfo.php files should go running showing something like this:

PHP Version 5.5.27

System	Windows NT PC-ANTONIO 6.2 build 9200 (Windows 8 Professional Edition) i586
Build Date	Jul 9 2015 12:09:00
Compiler	MSVC11 (Visual C++ 2012)
Architecture	x86
Configure Command	cscript /nologo configure.js "--enable-snapshot-build" "--disable-isapi" "--enable-debug-pack" "--without-mssql" "--without-pdo-mssql" "--without-pi3web" "--with-pdo-oci=C:\php-sdk\oracle\x86\instantclient10\sdk,shared" "--with-oci8=C:\php-sdk\oracle\x86\instantclient10\sdk,shared" "--with-oci8-11g=C:\php-sdk\oracle\x86\instantclient11\sdk,shared" "--enable-object-out-dir=../obj/" "--enable-com-dotnet=shared" "--with-mcrypt=static" "--disable-static-analyze" "--with-pgo"
Server API	Apache 2.0 Handler
Virtual Directory Support	enabled
Configuration File (php.ini) Path	C:\Windows
Loaded Configuration File	C:\xampp\php\php.ini
Scan this dir	(none)

The page is very long and shows the version php installed with all its attributes. In particular, through the document we are:

_SERVER["DOCUMENT_ROOT"]   D:/xampp/htdocs

_SERVER["REQUEST_SCHEME"]   http

_SERVER["CONTEXT_PREFIX"] no value

_SERVER["CONTEXT_DOCUMENT_ROOT"] D:/xampp/htdocs

_SERVER["SERVER_ADMIN"]   postmaster@localhost

_SERVER["SCRIPT_FILENAME"]D:/xampp/htdocs/dashboard/phpinfo.php

and that is where they will be inserted file.php file name.

The first php files

Start Notepad, and in a new document type:

```
<? Php
echo 'Ciao mondo';
?>
```

Save the file as 'prova.php' in the folder where the file phpinfo.php
Attention to the file suffix because Notepad saves .txt, if you have already done to change it in php.
Into your browser's address bar, type the address previously written replacing phpinfo.php with prova.php
(For example, http: //localhost/dashboard/prova.php)
In the browser you should see the "*Ciao Mondo*" message:
Now you can use the Apache web server locally,
create and test php applications using MySQL and more.

phpMyAdmin

Composed of Php scripts, allow you to manage the server on which it resides.
To do so you need to install the interpreter of PHP language and activate an Apache Web server, an operation that has been exposed in the previous pages.
phpMyAdmin is present practically on all Internet servers that offer php / MySQL learn using locally is also very useful and then use it anywhere.
The figure shows the access to phpMyAdmin page.

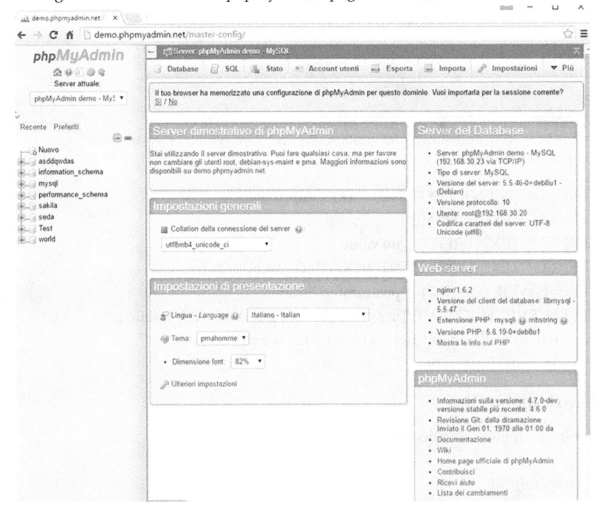

It is divided into two parts one on the left and the other on the right:

- The left, smaller in size, is present in all of phpMyAdmin pages.
  In this area you can read the names of the MySQL database on the server.
  Next to the name of each database, the number in parentheses indicates the number of tables contained in it.
  Clicking on the name of the table names are displayed.
- The right changes depending on the actions you intend to accomplish.
  At the top, a menu of choices to access phpMyAdmin services.
  The main choices are:
  - Create a new database (by specifying its name).
    - Once you create a new database entry / menu shows "Structure."
      Clicking on this page is displayed that describes the table structure with fields that comprise it and its features.
      Here you can change the table structure.
  - Export to export tables
  - Import to import tables
  - Operations to create or rename and copy tables.

Android apps and databases

Sometimes, in computer science, you may have the impression starting from the end parts for a project, but in order to interface an Android App with MySQL database tables must have these.
The first step is the creation of the database and then the tables contained in it.

Create database

Open a browser and in the address bar type:
http: // localhost / phpMyAdmin /

If the listening port has been changed, the address type would be:
http: // localhost: 81 / phpMyAdmin /
and any other number of selected target.

This will open the phpMyAdmin software

Click the Database button in the top menu.
It will open the window that contains the control where to insert the database name.
On the page that is displayed on the right side of the monitor to specify the name under the label "Create a new database" write "appinventor2".

The "character encoding" drop-down box can be left blank, will be the default options set.

Database

Click "Crea" button.

The "appinventor2" database will be created and its name added to the database in the left column of phpMyAdmin.

At this point the created database is empty.
This will open a window for creating a table.

Create tables

Once the database is created, it is empty, so you must create the tables that compose it.
To create a table, must specify the name and number of fields that comprise with their characteristics.
To do that you can click on the button "Options" in the top menu and the page that opens under the label "Create tables" type the name of the table and just below the number of fields.

In some versions of phpMyAdmin is a link "New" as the first item in the list of database tables.
In the control name, type the name of the table, ie "ai2tabella".
The number of proposed fields should be 4 if not, write 4 in the control "number of fields".

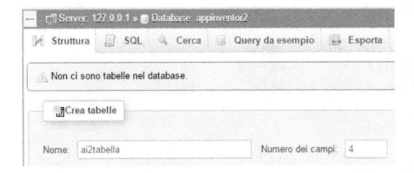

Click "Esegui" button.
The table name and quantity of the fields that make up has been defined.
Appear a mask for the placing of the names of the fields and the characteristics of each of them

Define the field properties

Among the configurable features, are important indexing a field, the uniqueness of its values.
These features are essential to the functioning of the App OS Androiid that will be interfaced with this table.
Important, but not essential, it is the inclusion of descriptive notes in the camps to facilitate understanding of the structure and future changes.

This is the definition of the fields of the table "ai2tabella":

- Appinventor2: database
  - ai2tabella: database table with four fields
    - id: number, primary key index (primary key).
      It allows you to uniquely identify each record in the table.
      Increased inclusion of each new record (AUTO_INCREMENT).
      In case of cancellation of a record the value will no longer be used.
      By means of identifying uniquely you can be accessed quickly and uniquely to each record
    - nome: varchar (20), 20-character string.
      VARCHAR, variable-length string, the real memory occupied in the database is equal to the length of text + 1
    - note: varchar (300), the string of 300 characters.
    - data: TIMESTAMP, automatically determines the instant at which a given record was entered or modified.

Graphically presents a scheme like the following figure

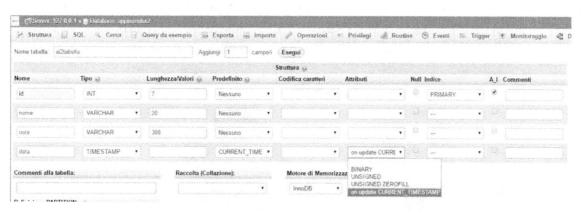

For some operations must point on boxes with the Tab key or use the horizontal scroll bar at the bottom of the page that allows access to the boxes that are not displayed.
The actual creation of a table is made by clicking the Save button.
Immediately after creation, phpMyAdmin will display a message that your creation and displays the structure.

For each table created above, you can have the structure editing page access by making it active, then clicking the Design button.

The fields, including their name, can be changed with the actions of any buttons Edit in the Action column.

Check tables

To see if the table structure has been defined properly, you must insert a few test data.

Click the Insert button, a window will open with two empty records, pending the entry of data.

- In both records leave the id field blank, it will increase to entering records.
- In the Name field, the Value column, write: Tuscany and Umbria in the first record in the second
- In the field notes, the Value column, write: Population 3692433 in the first record and the second record 889,497
- In both records leave the date field blank,
  automatically assume the instant when the record was entered (or modified in the future) in the format: year - month - day - hours - minutes – seconds

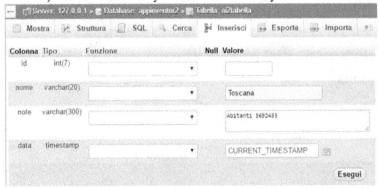

The actual placing of data is to click on the "Esegui" button.
Soon after, if there are no errors, the result is shown.

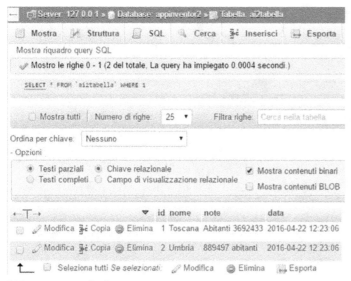

We can read above:

Show rows 0-1 (2 total, Query took 0.0004 seconds) and just below:
SELECT * FROM 'ai2tabella' WHERE 1
which is the SQL used to query that showed all records.

As we can see:

- The id field contains the values 1 and 2 respectively for the first and second record that the system added by performing the instructions given in the table definition.
- Field data of both record contains the value 2016-04-22 12:23:06 which means that the records were created in the year 2016, in the month 04=April, the day 22, 12 hours, 23 minutes and 06 seconds.

  These method of storing the time is very convenient because in the case of sorting the records on this field you do not need any other operation.

Correction of the content of the fields

The content of the record can be changed, it can be done here or later, by clicking the "SQL" button, by executing a query on the active table.
Once the records are on screen use the action buttons placed next to each record (edit, copy, delete).

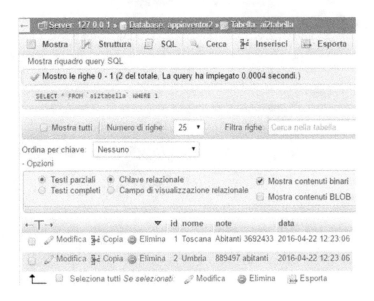

The same operations can be performed on multiple records by selecting the check mark in the bottom line.

Check the date field

A final check can be used to verify that the field will be updated as planned, then not only the inclusion of each new record, but also time the record is modified.
In view of all the records as in the previous image, click Edit the record with id = 2, that is Umbria.
In the window that appears, change the contents of the memo field by writing:
"Population 889 497" in place of the existing text, then click on the "Run" button.
Do now click the SQL button in the top bar, all records will be shown.
Check the date of the record field with id = 2, it should contain the date and time when the change was made.
Otherwise, view the table in Design mode, and write correctly the data field attributes.
In the example below the record with id = 2 has been changed by the system
2016, 04 month (April), day 22 to 12 hours, 25 minutes and 02 seconds. (Server time)

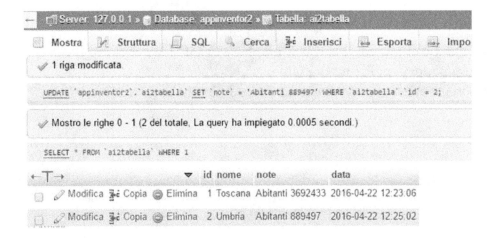

Querying a table

Each table can be queried by writing a SQL query in the window that appears when you click on "SQL" or "Search" in the command bar.

SQL method

By default is showed a selection query that all fields of the current table.
You must click on the "Esegui" button.

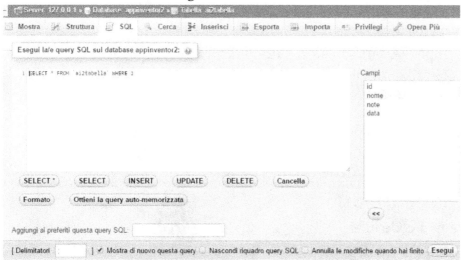

The list of records generated by the query is displayed in another window with the command that generated in a message like:

Showing rows 0 - 15 (16 of the total, Query took 0.0004 seconds.)

On the page you can edit the query executed by clicking the Edit button.

However, there is no syntax checking and is therefore only suitable and experienced SQL.

Search method

It is shown a page with the list of fields as in the next image.

In the Operator column, you can insert the search terms:
Major, Minor, LIKE etc.
Note that phpMyAdmin offers only the approved conditions for each field type, if more than one, click the drop-down menu of each field.

In the Value column must insert the researched value for each row.
The controls left blank will not be considered.
Write "**Toscana**" in the field name of control column Value
By clicking the " Esegui" button, the query is sent to execution.

With the inserted values phpMyAdmin creates, automatically in background, the query needed and executes it.
A window will open with a message like:

Show rows 0-0 (1 total, Query took 0.0004 seconds.)
and shown in the query in phpMyAdmin wrote, for example:
SELECT * FROM `ai2tabella` WHERE` name` LIKE 'Toscana'

On the same page clicking a button:
"Create php" code generates a code like:

$Sql = "SELECT * FROM` ai2tabella` WHERE `name` LIKE 'Tuscany' ';
you can use in your php pages
remarkable utility to gain familiarity with SQL.
Below is a list of records returned by a query executed.

Tables, copy, empty and delete

In phpMyAdmin, by clicking on the button "Transactions" you'll open the page where you can:

- Duplicate tables, copying them in the same or another database with the data or not.
- Delete all table record with the "Clear" button
- Delete tables with TRUNCATE command

Tables, import and export

To import tables from an external file to phpMyAdmin must click on the button "Import" or "Export" in a top menu.
For description see sections:

- Download from the local database tables

Load tables on the remote database

Connection to database

To let an application developed in PHP / MySQL could use the data contained in a database that must have access.
It seems a phrase taken for granted, but it is a task to be accomplished.
This is possible using a commonly called "pairing process".
To open the connection from PHP to MySQL database, it should be using the mysql_connect () function.
If successful, mysql_connect () returns a link identifier, otherwise it returns FALSE.

The connection requires parameter

- hostname: Name of the host machine.
  It uniquely identifies a location on the Web.
  It can be expressed as an IP address or string.
  In the case of local installation hostname it is usually called "localhost."
- username: Name of the user authorized to access and data manipulation.
  If the username local installation is generally called "root"
- password: The password that allows access to the database
- database: The database name

Generally these parameters then used to make the connection are inserted into variables.

A type of link could look like:

$ Hostname = "localhost";
$ Username = "root";
$ Password = "";
$ Database = "appinventor2";

$ Link = mysqli_connect ($ hostname, $ username, $ password, $ database);
if (mysqli_connect_errno ()) {echo "Connection failed". die (mysqli_connect_error ());}

Or in older versions but still used:

$ D = mysql_pconnect ($ hostname, $ username, $ password) or trigger_error (mysql_error (), E_USER_ERROR);

The different type of connection requires to use different types of query syntax.
Not to be confused with SQL syntax remains the same.

If it is used as dated code, the one contained in the sample pages downloaded it in their name have AI2- (hyphen), you should have an answer like:

*Deprecated: mysql_pconnect (): The mysql extension is deprecated and will be removed in the future: use mysqli or PDO instead in **D: \ inetpub \ webs \ servername \ ai2-connessionedb.php** on line xy*

Both versions can be downloaded from the author's website.

Connection scripts

In My Computer, go to the folder:
C:\xampp\htdocs\dashboard (the one containing phpinfo.php)
and create a folder named "AI2".
The "AI2" folder will contain all the necessary php pages to App_Web_PHP_MySQL operation.
The same order of the folders will then be played on servers in the Internet.

Open Notepad and write the text of the underlying script between <? Php and?> I included.
Save the page in the folder C: \ xampp \ htdocs \ dashboard \ AI2
as ai2-connessionedb.php
The folder may be different from the dashboard, it is one where the php test was approved (see section php test).

Pay attention to the file's suffix because the Windows Notepad saves .txt : possibly after saving, change the suffix from .txt to php or the script does not work.

This page will work with both local and remote databases.

```php
<?php
//echo 'SERVER_NAME = '.$_SERVER['SERVER_NAME']."<br>";
if ($_SERVER['SERVER_NAME'] == 'localhost') {
//echo" They are locally ";
$hostname = "localhost";
$username = "root";
$password = "";
$database = "appinventor2";
$NomeConnessione = mysql_pconnect($hostname, $username, $password) or
trigger_error(mysql_error(),E_USER_ERROR);
}
else
{
//echo" sono in remoto - remotely ";
$hostname = "11.222.333.444";
$username = "Sql999999";
$password = "abcdefghijk";
$database = "appinventor2";
$NomeConnessione = mysql_pconnect($hostname, $username, $password) or
trigger_error(mysql_error(),E_USER_ERROR);
}
?>
<?php // stringa di connessione
mysql_select_db($database, $NomeConnessione);
?>

<?php // executing the query to display the contents of the table
/*
$query = "Select ai2tabella.id, ai2tabella.nome, ai2tabella.note, ai2tabella.data From
ai2tabella ";
$result = mysql_query($query) or die ("Quesry failed; " .mysql_error());
while ($row = mysql_fetch_array($result))
{echo "<br>".$row['id'], " - " , $row['nome'], " - " , $row['note'], " - " , $row['data'];}
*/
?>
```

Once complete, open the browser and in the address bar write:
http://localhost:81/dashboard/AI2/ai2-connessionedb.php

Without ":81" if you have not changed the port and replacing it if the port number is different.
Same thing for the dashboard folder, if it is a different folder enter the proper name.
You should see a page completely white, testing has been successful. If you want to see what can be read, it is possible to make a further test, the downloaded file also contains the code:

```
<?php // esecuzione della query per visualizzare il contenuto della tabella
//executing the query to display the contents of the table
/*
$query = "Select ai2tabella.id, ai2tabella.nome, ai2tabella.note, ai2tabella.data From ai2tabella ";
$result = mysql_query($query) or die ("Quesry failed; " .mysql_error());
while ($row = mysql_fetch_array($result))
{echo "<br>".$row['id'], " - " , $row['nome'], " - " , $row['note'], " - " , $row['data'];}
*/
?>
```

Remove / * and * /, save and revive, should appear on the monitor the contents of the table "ai2tabella" similar to:
1 - Toscana - Abitanti 3692433 - 2016-04-22 12:23:06
2 - Umbria - Abitanti 889497 - 2016-04-22 12:25:02

....

....

The database name $database can not always be chosen, sometimes is imposed by the Internet provider.
Obviously the connection data for the remote database are fictional

Insert, modify and delete with php

The phpMyAdmin software is a graphical interface that allows you to directly manage databases and tables contained in them.
With phpMyAdmin you can view the contents of the database, create, modify and delete tables and / or individual records, make backups, view information about the database components etc.
phpMyAdmin is a very useful tool for anyone, even esparto php / MySQL, want to create or speed tests on the database that is implementing.

But once with phpMyAdmin everything is tested and ready for use, including the connection script, for database management operations must be something usable also be viewed by non-programmers.

A script that turns on the Internet and password authorized persons can enter, modify, delete records without knowing the commands underlying these operations.

For these operations, the scripts presented in this guide is ai2-gestionedati.php

Because this script is intended to run on the Internet, in order to have access to and manage it, it will implement other two pages (downloadable from the author's site):

- **ai2-index.php**: This page will be access through Username and Password entry with subsequent confirmation by clicking on a button.
  If username and password are correct you will set the $ _SESSION ['session variable access'], and the user will be redirected to **ai2-gestionedati.php** page.
  - o The $ _SESSION ['accesso'] session variable is able to keep track of choices and data transmitted between client and server.
    This mechanism keeps track of previous selections made by the user (user name and password, type it exactly).
- **ai2-accessosessione.php**: This page is tested,
  (after each operation in **ai2-gestionedati.php**)
  the session variable $ _SESSION ['access']
  If $ _SESSION ['access'] does not contain the values fit the script
  ai2-gestionedati.php cease referring to ai2-index.php page.

An internal mechanism to this page tests if the script is locally or on the Internet and acts only in the second case.

The command includes php require_once

With PHP, like any other programming language, you may have to run several times the same code that performs a particular job.
To not have to retype the commands include or require permit to include a page within another (the one containing include or require).
The contents of the included page is positioned at the point where the command appears.
The differences between include() and require_once() you can see when the code is included multiple times or the page you want to include is not found, but the detailed description is beyond the scope of this guide.

In these scripts the inclusion is done:

- From *ai2-gestionedati.php* page:
  - **ai2-connessionedb.php**, database connection
  - **ai2-accessosessione.php**, variable head $ _SESSION ['access']
- From **ai2-interfaccia.php** page:
  - **ai2-connessionedb.php** database connection

ai2-gestionedati.php

The page code is simplified as much as possible by eliminating what is beyond the mere functioning. The page must be in the "AI2" folder and can be edited with Windows Notepad.
This page includes 3 forms that refer to the same page and 2 functions.

- formNUOVO: Inserting new record.
  Communicate the name of the region to be inserted.
  Nell'inserimenti, the system adds an id index for the new record.
  It is activated when you click on button id = "button3"
- formMODIFICA: Notify id index of the record to which make the changes, changes to be made to the fields.
  If the record was just inserted, it allows you to complete it.
  It is activated when you click on button id = "button"
- formELIMINA: Notify index id of the record to be deleted.
  It is activated when you click on button id = "button2"

- Addslashes() function puts a backslash (\) to all characters that may interfere with the proper performance of a query.
  These characters are: single quote, double quote, backslash, NUL
- Stripslashes() function performs the inverse work addslashes ()

Code commented ai2-dati.php management

```
<?php include('ai2-accessosessione.php'); ?>
<?php require_once('ai2-connessionedb.php'); ?>

<?php // NuovoRecord  - Record new
/*
The command: $sql = "INSERT INTO ai2tabella (nome) VALUES ('$ nomeNEW')";
inserts the new record with the value of the variable $ nomeNEW in the Name field.
As established in the table definition, the new record is assigned a new id index
Automatically, that is unique and progressive value.
*/
$nomeNEW = addslashes(isset($_POST['nomeNEW']) ? $_POST['nomeNEW'] : 0);
if(strlen($nomeNEW)>3)
```

```php
{
$query = "INSERT INTO ai2tabella (nome) VALUES ('$nomeNEW')";
$result = mysql_query($query) or die ("Quesry failed; " .mysql_error());
}
?>
```

```php
<?php // modifica  - modification
/*
Changing an existing record.
This happens when you click on id = "button" button formMODIFICA form, passing the id
index of records contained in the variable $ idmodifica.
if ($idmodifica> 0), which controls $ idmodifica has a value greater than zero.
If so in the variables $nome and $note values are entered for the quey modification of the
record.
The command: $sql ="UPDATE ai2tabella SET nome = '$nome', note = '$note' WHERE id =
$idmodifica";
inserts the new value in the fields of ai2tabella table id of records whose value is contained
in the variable $idmodifica
*/
$idmodifica = isset($_POST['idmodifica']) ? $_POST['idmodifica'] : 0;
if($idmodifica > 0)
{
        $nome = addslashes(isset($_POST['nome']) ? $_POST['nome'] : "no nome");
        $note = addslashes(isset($_POST['note']) ? $_POST['note'] : "no note");
$query = "UPDATE ai2tabella SET nome = '$nome', note = '$note' WHERE id =
$idmodifica ";
$result = mysql_query($query) or die ("Quesry failed; " .mysql_error());
}
?>
```

```php
<?php // cancella  - delete
/*
Delete a record.
This happens when you click on id = "button2" button formELIMINA form, passing the
index id of the record to be deleted.
if ($ idcancella> 0), check that the $idcancella has a value greater than zero.
The command: $sql =" DELETE FROM ai2tabella WHERE id = $idcancella "
deletes the record whose value is contained in the variable $idcancella
*/
$idcancella = isset($_POST['idcancella']) ? $_POST['idcancella'] : 0;
if($idcancella > 0)
{
$query = "DELETE FROM ai2tabella WHERE id = $idcancella ";
$result = mysql_query($query) or die ("Quesry failed; " .mysql_error());
}
?>
```

```php
<?php // legge tabella  - read table
/*
the query is created to display the record, then sent running. The result is in the variable
$result
*/
$query = "Select ai2tabella.id, ai2tabella.nome, ai2tabella.note, ai2tabella.data From
ai2tabella";
$result = mysql_query($query) or die ("Quesry failed; " .mysql_error());
?>


<!doctype html>
<html>
<head>
<!--
codifica dei caratteri con vocali accentate ecc. e titolo pagina
page encoding characters
-->
<meta charset="utf-8">
<title>-Gestione dati</title>
<!--
Commands CSS who eat the page and center the text
-->
<style type="text/css">
body {margin-left: 0px;margin-top: 0px;margin-right: 0px;margin-bottom: 0px; text-
align:center;}
</style>
</head>

<body>
<!--
Inizio tabella che conterrà i dati, essa è larga il 100% del suo contenitore ed io bordo di 1
pixel.
Start table that contains the data, it is wide the 100% of its container and the edge of 1 pixel
-->
<table width="100%" border="1">

<!--
The first row of the tag between <tr table> and </ tr> identifiable beginning and end of a
line, the tags between <td> and </ td> identify the beginning and end of a cell
-->
<tr><td> </td><td>

<!--
form to the insertion of a new record, method = "post" is the method of data transition,
action = "" recalls the same page
-->
 <form name="formNUOVO" method="post" action="">
```

```
<!--
```
Pulsante per l'invio dei dati, id="button3" è l'identificativo, value="Nuovo record" è il testo che può essere letto sul pulsante
Button to send data, id = "button3" is the identifier, value = "Nuovo record" is the text that can be read on the button
```
-->
 <input type="submit" name="button3" id="button3" value="Nuovo record">
 <br>
<!--
```
Text that will be sent to be entered in the Name field of the new record. The text will be sent content id = "nomeNEW" whose value will have to be entered by the user in the value = ""
```
-->
 <input name="nomeNEW" type="text" id="nomeNEW">

 </form>

 </td><td> </td><td> </td><td> </td></tr>

<!--
```
Seconda riga della tabella con intestazione delle colonne/campi
The second line of the table with column headers/fields
```
-->

<tr><td>modifica</td><td>nome</td><td>note</td><td>data</td><td>cancella</td></tr>

<?php
/*
```
Beginning of the reading of the record with the while loop.
Each record is read in $row and decomposed in fields $row['id'] - $row['nome'] - $row['note'] - $row['data'] and then inserted in the corresponding controls.
The number of rows is generated by PHP in the exact quantity to contain all records.
```
```
*/
while ($row = mysql_fetch_array($result))
{
// Reading fields, not visible on the page because preceded by //
//echo $row['id']." - ".$row['nome']." - ".$row['note']." - ".$row['data']. "<br>";
?>

<!--
```
Third row start lines for records beginning formMODIFICA form, method="post" is the method of passing data, action="" recalls the same page
```
-->
 <tr><form name="formMODIFICA" method="post" action="">
 <td>
```
```

```
<!--
Pulsante per l'invio dei dati del record da modificare
-->
<input type="submit" name="button" id="button" value="modifica">
```

```
<!--
Identifier for the modification of the record is the id="idmodifica".
To load the page value="0", in the generation of the row of the page value assumes the id
value of the record represented.
-->
<input name="idmodifica" type="text" id="idmodifica" value="<?php echo $row['id']
?>">
</td>
```

```
<!--
The second cell to the field name, value assumes the value of a field of the record
represented.
-->
<td><input name="nome" type="text" id="nome" value="<?php echo
stripslashes($row['nome']) ?>"></td>
```

```
<!--
The third cell for the Notes field, value assumes the value of a field of the record
represented.
-->
<td><textarea name="note" id="note"><?php echo stripslashes($row['note'])
?></textarea></td>
```

```
<!--
Fourth cell for the field date (year, month, day, hours, minutes, seconds), value assumes
the value of a field of the record represented.
This value is entered as the moment of creation of the record and changes at the time of his
every change
-->
<td><?php echo $row['data'] ?></td>
</form>
```

```
<!--
The fifth cell for the Field Delete method="post" is the method of passing data, action=""
recalls the same page
-->
<td><form name="formELIMINA" method="post" action="">
```

```
<!--
Button for sending data of the record to delete
-->
<input type="submit" name="button2" id="button2" value="cancella">
```

```
<!--
Identifier for the modification of the record is id=" idcancella ".
To load the page value="0", in the generation of the row of the page value assumes the
value of the id of the record represented.
-->
<input name="idcancella" type="text" id="idcancella" value="<?php echo $row['id'] ?>">
</form></td>
</tr>
<?php
}
/*
The end of the cycle of the while loop. Each loop has created a new line of the table
containing a record
*/
?>
</table>
</body>
</html>
```

Like all the other php pages must be inside the folder AI2
Open a browser and type in the address bar,

http://localhost: 81/dashboard/AI2/ai2-gestionedati.php

or at least the valid address for the ragging ai2-gestionedati.php page
Result of running code:

ai2-index.php

This page is accessed by entering the Username and Password with subsequent
confirmation by clicking on a button.
With exact username and Password get sets the vaiable $_SESSION ['session variable
access'], and the user will be redirected to ai2-gestionedati.php page described above.

With the $ _SESSION ['access'] session variable is kept track of by the user choices made in this case username and password.
The page contains one form to capture usernames and passwords, which refers to the page itself.

Username and password are checked and if they match those set is launched session_start (); and crated the session variable $ _SESSION ['access'] = 'ok';

Immediately after the user is redirected to the page with ai2-gestionedati.php

echo '<META HTTP-EQUIV = "REFRESH" CONTENT = "0; URL = i2-gestionedati.php">';

Page ai2-gestionedati.php described previously.

If User Name or Password are not those established, the page is reloaded listening for a new insertion of username and password.

Code commented ai2-index.php

```php
<?php
/*
Riceve username e Password.
Naturalmente al primo avvio le variabili sono vuote e quindi la pagina viene caricata
completamente e messa in attesa dell'immissione di Username e Password

A username and password.
When you first start the variables are empty and then the page loads completely and put
on hold by placing Username and Password
*/
$Username = isset($_POST['Username']) ? $_POST['Username'] : "";
$Password = isset($_POST['Password']) ? $_POST['Password'] : "";

/*
Username and Password head,
if you have to be exact Username = "MiaUsername" and Password = "MyPassword"
Changing "MiaUsername" and "MyPassword" can be customized and replaced with the
ones you want.
*/
if ($Username == "MiaUsername" and $Password = "MiaPassword")
{
/*
If the test is successful is launched session_start (), created the session variable $
_SESSION [ 'access'] = 'ok';
```

assigning a value to be tested during the boots of ai2-gestionedati.php page

the user is redirected to the real-ai2 gestionedati.php page
*/

```
session_start ();
$_SESSION['accesso'] = "ok";
echo '<META HTTP-EQUIV="REFRESH" CONTENT="0; URL=ai2-gestionedati.php">';
}
?>

<!doctype html>
<html>
<head>
<meta charset="utf-8">
<title>-AI2 e PHP/MySQL</title>

<style type="text/css">
/* CSS commands that format the page and text*/
body {margin-left: 0px;margin-top: 0px;margin-right: 0px;margin-bottom: 0px;
font:Arial, Helvetica, sans-serif; font-size:12px; }
table {font-size: 80%;align:left; valign:top;}
</style>

</head>

<body>

<?php
/*
Reads the current date on the server, this is not necessary to the operation of the page, but
only demonstration of data / management zones which will then be used in the records.
*/
$giorno = date("j"); $mese = date("n"); $anno = date("Y"); $ora = date("H:i"); $settimana =
date("w");
$giornosettimana = array ("Domenica", "Lunedi", "Martedi", "Mercoledi","Giovedi",
"Venerdi", "Sabato");
$nomemese = array (1 => "gennaio", "febbraio", "marzo", "aprile","maggio", "giugno",
"luglio", "agosto", "settembre", "ottobre", "novembre", "dicembre");
echo ("$giornosettimana[$settimana]" . " " . "$giorno" . " " . "$nomemese[$mese]" . " " .
"$anno")." ore $ora ";
?>

<br>Inserire username e password

<!--
Form for capturing username and password, method = "post" is the method of data
transition, action = "" calls the same page.
-->
```

```
<form name="form1" method="post" action="">

<!--
The Username text that will be sent to be tested will be contained in id = "Username"
whose value will have to be entered by the user in the value = ""
-->
<input type="password" name="Username" id="Username"><br>

<!--
The Password text that will be sent to be tested will be contained in id = "Password" the
value of which shall be entered by the user in the value = ""
-->
<input type="password" name="Password" id="Password"><br>

<!--
Button to send data, id = "button" is the identifier, value = "Login" is the text that can be
read on the button
-->
<input type="submit" name="button" id="button" value="Accedi">
</form>
</body>
</html>
```

Like all the other php pages must be inside the folder AI2
Open a browser and type in the address bar,

http://localhost:81/dashboard/AI2/ai2-index.php

or at least the valid address where ai2-index.php page
Result of running code:

AI2 e PHP/MySQL

Lunedì 16 maggio 2016 ore 18:29
Inserire username e password

Accedi

ai2-accessosessione.php

This page, which must be within the "AI2" folder, check that the session variable (the one assigned after the 'Username and password entry has valid content).

Code commented ai2-access sessione.php

```php
<?php
session_start(); // Starts the session
/*
Type server, local or internet
echo 'SERVER_NAME = '.$_SERVER['SERVER_NAME']."<br>";
Tests whether locally, if positive result does not head the session variable
*/
if ($_SERVER['SERVER_NAME'] == 'localhost'){}
else // otherwise
{
/*
Head the $ _SESSION [ 'access'] session variable, if it contains "ok" refer to i2-index.php
page to ask insertion of username and password.
*/
if($_SESSION['accesso'] <> "ok")
{echo '<META HTTP-EQUIV="REFRESH" CONTENT="0; URL=ai2-index.php">';}
}
?>
```

Android App interface with MySQL database

Now we have, locally, a working server with MySQL database, php pages to protect, enter, edit and delete records, you must select the page that the table data and at the same time is the interface with the App_Web_PHP_MySQL Operating System Android assembled with App Inventor

This interface will be named "**ai2-interfaccia.php**".

The data selection so it has already been seen in **ai2-gestionedati.php** file with the code:

```php
<?php
// query execution to display table
$query = "Select ai2tabella.id, ai2tabella.nome, ai2tabella.note, ai2tabella.data From ai2tabella";
```

```
$result = mysql_query($query) or die ("Quesry failed; " .mysql_error());
echo $row['id']." - ".$row['nome']." - ".$row['note']." - ".$row['data']. "<br>";
?>
```

They are read and showed all records of the table and all fields in each record, without any kind of order they 'content filtering.

To do it App_Web_PHP_MySQL on Android device, by imposing on sort fields and selection, you must choose a method for passing the commands between App_Web_PHP_MySQL and "ai2-interfaccia.php".
Pick the one you need to define some rules that operate with the method chosen by ensuring that App_Web_PHP_MySQL and "ai2-interfaccia.php" can communicate with each other.

For the passage of commands from the App to the php page on the Internet server was chosen the query-string method.

query-string

A query-string is the part of a URL (Internet address) containing the data to be passed as input to a program, in this case to a web page in php format.

In the example are used php pages, but it is not the only possible, for example javascript can handle the query-string, and then, on the page, go eg. with AJAX technology.

By App, The URL query-string must contain the complete address for attaining the web page in Internet.
At the end of the URL, the sign of "?" opens the query-string.
The commands passed to the query-string does not include the sign "?", But everything that follows it.

Being implemented in all browsers and scripting languages, the syntax of the query-string is a de facto standard, it follows the following pattern:

- Question mark ?
- Parameter1 = 1 value parameter2 = value2 & parameter3 value = 3

Each parameter is assigned a value by using the "=" sign.
The parameters are interspersed with each other by the symbol "&"

The HTTP protocol does not provide the URL length limits, although some browsers restrict this length to about 2000 characters, however, more than enough for interface purposes.

The number of parameters is therefore only limited by the length of the query-string accepted the browser that will receive.

If the query-string exceeds the allowed length of the receiving browser, there are no mistakes usually, only that the excess values are ignored.

Some alphabetic characters have unique meaning when used within the query-string. There is no real limitation on their use, but in the planning of query-string are best avoided because they create ambiguities and in any case should be coded before they are used.

- **Reserved characters in query-string:**
  Inside URLs, some characters have specific functions and to avoid conflicts it is best not to use them or, alternatively, must be encoded before transmission.
  The reserved characters are: $ - & - + -, - / -: -; - = -? - @ (The hyphen - here used as a room divider is allowed)
  Other characters may create ambiguity and is not advisable to use, they are:
  "" (Space) "" "(quotes)" < ""> "" # ""% ", however it is better to use them to encode them before transmission.
- **UrlEncode Encoding:**
  In the encoding, each character to be encoded, it is replaced by a triplet composed by "%" followed by two characters representing the hexadecimal value.
  For example:% 20 represents a space,% 24 represents the $ symbol and so on.
  The space can also be represented by the symbol "+", a shorthand notation used to make the query-string interpreted even by those systems that do not support spaces.

To make the code more understandable in App_Web_PHP_MySQL, for communication between this and "ai2-interface" has been made sure not to use reserved characters.

ai2-interfaccia.php

The interface code is divided into three sections.
Common section:
A) It connects to the database
B) Defines the label for the field names and sorting
C) receives commands and values with the query-string.
The query-string receives the command to which of sections 1 and 2 to execute.
section 1
Select and filter data
section 2
Returns the contents of the requested records

Tasks and rules interface

The table "ai2tabella" has 4 fields, the App can be controlled by:

- Order in ascending or descending order any of the fields of the table.
- Filter, that is, select, records in the table of a field.
  To do this the App will send the identifier of a field and the search string.
    - The text will be matched anywhere in the identified field.
    - we'll show you all the records that have that text field in the filtrate.
- Return to App_Web_PHP_MySQL the content of the requested records.

Interface variables

Variables that will receive the values as query-string from App_Web_PHP_MySQL:

- $IO: number with value 1 or 2, corresponding to the section to be used.
  If $IO = 1: must be running section 1, select and filter data
  If $IO = 2: goes running section 2, returns content records requested
- $N: field number (0 to 3) on which to sort the records that will be filtered
- $T: sort order a-z or z-a
- $C: column / field (0 to 3) on which to apply the filter
- $F: filter to apply on the field $ C
- $id: the index whose records contained is to be returned to App_Web_PHP_MySQL

Code commented ai2-interfaccia.php

```php
// collegamento al database
// Database Connection
<?php require_once('ai2-connessionedb.php'); ?>

<?php
// nomi dei campi e tipo ordinamento
// Field names and sort order
$Campo = array("id","nome","note","data");
$TipoOrdinamento = array("", "Desc");
$CampoRicerca = array("id","nome","note","data");
?>

<?php
// Input Output 1=selezione/filtraggio 2=restituisce il record id
// Input Output 1 = selection / filtering 2 = returns the record id

$IO = isset($_GET['IO']) ? $_GET['IO'] : 0;
```

```php
// per array $Campo[] : numero del campo sul quale ordinare (da 0 a 3)
// Array $Campo[]: number of the field on which to order (0 to 3)
$N = isset($_GET['N']) ? $_GET['N'] : 1;


// per array $TipoOrdinamento[] : tipo ordinamento a-z oppure z-a (Desc)
// Array type $ Order []: Sorting type a-z or z-a (Desc)
$T = isset($_GET['T']) ? $_GET['T'] : 0;


// per array $CampoRicerca[] : colonna/campo sul quale applicare il filtro (da 0 a 3)
// Array $ Campo search []: column / field on which to filter (0 to 3)
$C = isset($_GET['C']) ? $_GET['C'] : 2;


// filtro da applicare sul campo $CampoRicerca[]
// Filter to apply on the field $ Field Research []
$F = isset($_GET['F']) ? $_GET['F'] : "%";


// id del record richiesto (se $IO == 2)
// Id of the requested record (if $ IO == 2)
$id = isset($_GET['id']) ? $_GET['id'] : 0;


/*
Restituisce una stringa con backslash
prima dei caratteri che compromettono l'esecuzione di una query
la funzione rende la query utilizzabile anche con i caratteri
apostrofo ( ' ), doppie virgolette ( " ), barra rovesciata ( \ ) e NUL.
funzione stripslashes() compie il lavoro inverso di addslashes()
viene usata sui dati letti dalla tabella prima di usarli

Returns a string with a backslashes
first character that affect the execution of a query
the function makes the query can also be used with the characters
apostrophe ( '), double quote ( "), backslash (\) and NUL.
stripslashes () function performs the inverse work addslashes ()
It is used on the data read from the table before you use them
*/
$F = addslashes($F);
?>


<?php
// sezione 1
// Section 1
/*
Ordina in senso ascendente o discendente uno qualsiasi dei campi in della tabella.
Filtra i record della tabella di un qualsiasi campo.
Il testo è cercato in un punto qualsiasi del campo identificato
Verranno mostrati tutti i record che nel campo filtrato hanno quel testo.
```

Sort in ascending or descending order any of the fields in the table.
Filter records in the table of a field.
The text is searched at any point of the identified field
We will show all records that have that text field in the filtrate.

```php
*/
if($IO == 1)
{
// esecuzione della query per visualizzare tabella
// Execute the query to display the table
$query = "Select ai2tabella.id, ai2tabella.nome, ai2tabella.note, ai2tabella.data
From ai2tabella
Where ai2tabella.".$CampoRicerca[$C]." Like '%".$F."%'
Order By ai2tabella.".$Campo[$N]." ".$TipoOrdinamento[$T];

// esecuzione della query risultato in $result
// Execution of the query result in $result
$result = mysql_query($query) or die ("Quesry failed; " .mysql_error());
?>
```

```html
<!doctype html>
<html>
<head>
<meta charset="utf-8">
<title>-Selezione dati</title>
<style type="text/css">
/*
Comandi CSS che formattano pagina e testo
CSS commands that format the page and text
*/
body {margin-left: 0px;margin-top: 0px;margin-right: 0px;margin-bottom: 0px;
font:Arial, Helvetica, sans-serif; font-size:12px; }
table {font-size: 80%;align:left; valign:top;}
</style>
</head>

<body>
<table width="100%" border="1">
<!--
nomi delle colonne/campi della tabella
names of the columns / fields of the table
-->
<tr><td>id</td><td>nome</td><td>note</td><td>data</td></tr>
```

```php
<?php
// loop sul risultato della query
// Loop on the result of the query
while ($row = mysql_fetch_array($result))
```

```
{
//echo $row['id']." - ".$row['nome']." - ".$row['note']." - ".$row['data']. "<br>";
// mette i record sul display
// Puts the records on the display
?>
 <tr>
  <td align="left" valign="top"><?php echo $row['id'] ?></td>
  <td align="left" valign="top"><?php echo stripslashes($row['nome']) ?></td>
  <td align="left" valign="top"><?php echo stripslashes($row['note']) ?></td>
  <td align="left" valign="top"><?php echo $row['data'] ?></td>
 </tr>
<?php
}
?>
</table>
</body>
</html>
<?php
}
?>


<?php
// sezione 2
// Section 2
// Restituisce il contenututo dei record richiesti
// Returns the contents of the requested records
if($IO == 2)
{
// codice della query
// Query code
$query = "Select ai2tabella.id, ai2tabella.nome, ai2tabella.note, ai2tabella.data
From ai2tabella
Where ai2tabella.id = $id ";

// esegue la query
// Run the query
$result = mysql_query($query) or die ("Quesry failed; " .mysql_error());
$QuantitaRecord = mysql_num_rows($result); // quantità record

if($QuantitaRecord > 0) // se il record c'è
{
$Record = mysql_fetch_assoc($result);
/*
inserisce il contenuto del record nella variabile
da usare per trasmetterne il contenuto
inserts the contents of the records in the variable
to use to transmit the content
```

```
*/
$testo =
$Record['id']."\n".stripslashes($Record['nome'])."\n".stripslashes($Record['note'])."\n".stri
pslashes($Record['data']);
}
else // otherwise
{
$testo = "Il record $id non esiste";
}
echo $testo; // trasmette alla App Android il contenuto del record
// It transmits to the content of the record Android App
}
?>
```

The esecution of Section 2 deals with the App and transmit the required records.
The request by the App "App_Web_PHP_MySQL" happens in the Web Component of
App inventor that trasmit the id of the record that wants to receive.
If the record does not exist, the page "ai2-interfaccia.php" responds with:
"The record $ id does not exist"

Test ai2-interfaccia.php locally

Open a browser and type in the address bar,

http://localhost:81/dashboard/AI2/ai2-interfaccia.php
or at least the valid address where ai2-interfaccia.php page
should load a blank page.
This means that the code works because dafault code:
$IO = isset($_GET['IO']) ? $_GET['IO'] : 0;
It assumes in the variable $IO to zero and then do not run any of the two subsequent
sections.

Make check-test

To change
$IO = isset($_GET['IO']) ? $_GET['IO'] : 0;
with
$IO = isset($_GET['IO']) ? $_GET['IO'] : 1;
and save the page.
Open a browser and in the address bar type the address where ai2-interfaccia.php page
The execution of section 1 of the result should look like this

id	nome	note	data
1	Toscana	Abitanti 3692433	2016-04-23 10:46:57
2	Umbria	Abitanti 889497	2016-04-22 12:25:02

To change
$IO = isset($_GET['IO']) ? $_GET['IO'] : 0;
with
$IO = isset($_GET['IO']) ? $_GET['IO'] : 2;
and save the page.
Open a browser and in the address bar, type the address for the ragging ai2-interfaccia.php page
It should see a result like this:

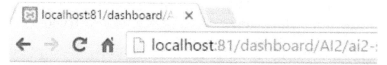

Il record 0 non esiste

It means that everything is in place because the line in the page:
$id = isset($_GET['id']) ? $_GET['id'] : 0;
assumes by default the transmission to zero records App, then look for and not finding answers:
"Il record 0 non esiste" - "The record does not exist 0"

Change the code
$id = isset($_GET['id']) ? $_GET['id'] : 0;
with
$id = isset($_GET['id']) ? $_GET['id'] : XX;

where XX is the id value for an existing record, save the page and update.
If everything is in place, it will appear on screen the contents of that record.

Storing data in the table with php

Now that the interface between the Android app and the php / MySQL database table is ready you must enter the "real" data in the table and then load everything on the Internet. The best thing is to do it locally so that, in case of errors, it is easier to spot them and correct them.
Launch ai2 gestionedati.php-file for example by typing in the browser bar;
Type http://localhost:81/dashboard/ai2-gestionedati.php
Will be stored names of some Italian regions and a brief description of each of them.

Contents of the records in the downloadable table.

id	nome	note	data
1	Toscana	La Toscana è una regione italiana di 3692433 abitanti, situata nell'Italia centrale, con capoluogo Firenze.	2015-11-09 15:25:32
2	Umbria	L'Umbria è una regione dell'Italia centrale di 889497 abitanti posta nel cuore della penisola.	2014-09-10 09:32:02
3	Piemonte	Il Piemonte è una regione dell'Italia nord-occidentale di 4.377.791 abitanti con capoluogo Torino.	2016-05-08 09:10:11
4	Val d'Aosta	La Valle d'Aosta (in francese: Vallée d'Aoste), con capoluogo Aosta, ha superficie di 3 263 kmq e 127562 abitanti.	2013-12-11 10:09:08
5	Sicilia	La Sicilia, ufficialmente Regione Siciliana, è una regione italiana autonoma a statuto speciale di 4995543 abitanti, con capoluogo Palermo.	2016-06-14 14:01:23
6	Sardegna	Regione italiana a statuto speciale insieme con le isole e gli arcipelaghi che la circondano è estesa 24100 kmq ha 1658649 abitanti distribuiti in 377 comuni.	2016-01-02 03:40:05
7	Basilicata	La Basilicata o anche comunemente Lucania è una regione dell'Italia Meridionale di 575 230 abitanti e ha come capoluogo Potenza.	2014-05-09 07:36:01
8	Lazio	Regione italiana a statuto ordinario dell'Italia Centrale di 5891582 abitanti. Capoluogo e capitale d'Italia è Roma.	2015-04-07 18:15:25

Load the Internet database and php pages

Locally everything is quite simple and if you followed the directions on the local server and pages should work perfectly.

Some difficulties may occur, for safety reasons, when the database is the Internet.

Most providers allow access to databases located on their servers only on requests from IP considered reliable, and one of the characteristics of reliability is that the addresses sourced from the same provider.

Eg. if you want a remote database server on Aruba, the interface between the app and the database server must be on Aruba and this is true for nearly every webserver.

Each web server has its own characteristics but they all look alike, and eg. have phpMyAdmin and support php4 / php5 + database, some are free.

In fact, there is free and you pay in different ways such as. advertising on their pages.

Among these we mention three where at the moment (spring 2016) in the first two the cost performance ratio is excellent, and the third "free".

Name and domain suffix must of course be chosen to make available, the price may vary with the type of suffix (it, com, net, etc.).

- Aruba (https://www.aruba.it/), based in Arezzo, is one of the Italian market leader for domains, hosting, cloud etc.
  A domain type http: //www.nomescelto.ext with unlimited space you can have about 30 euros per year and with another 10 €, five databases.
  Occasionally it has very competitive offers with even lower prices.
  Name of the database and password assigned by Aruba.
- One.com (https://www.one.com/it/) based in Denmark, a domain name like http: //www.nomescelto.ext with 15 GB of space you can have on less than 25 euro to including database 'year.
  From time to time they are also done very competitive offers for free domains by delivering predetermined periods of time.
  Database name and password assigned by one.com
- Altervista (http://it.altervista.org/) houses one of the largest web community of publishers who publish their own content on the Internet and it's free.
  You can decide whether to host on their pages one or more advertising campaigns, one supplied by the provider. The proceeds will be divided between the owner of the site and AlterVista. The insertion of advertising is not mandatory.

Get a domain with database

The following example refers to the Aruba servers, not very dissimilar from the others.

Go on the website Aruba https://www.aruba.it/ page, here you can type a domain name by choosing the suffix.
Once clicked enter or the search button, it will last a database and communicated the outcome.
If the domain name is free they will be presented in sequence a few pages where they are offered similar names and additional services that are not able, among them choose MySQL database.
At the end you are sought registration of their data in order to assign the domain and issue an invoice.
Payment can be done in various ways, PayPal, Credit cards, money transfer etc. Done the payment by e-mail you are disclosed parameters for access to the domain via ftp (File Transfer Protocol - file transfer protocol), 5 of database names and passwords.

Download tables from the local database

Once you choose your provider and you have dominoes and database, you need to load them on the Internet.
The php pages are already on your PC while the database and the table contained in it is located on the local server.
Since you can not directly transfer tables from the local database to the database for networking, "download" the table from the local server on your PC and then transfer it to the database hosted by the provider.

To do this, access to phpMyAdmin on the local server by typing:
http: // localhost: 81/phpMyAdmin /
eventually appropriate with the appropriate server port.

In the left column click on "appinventor2" database which get opened.
Click on the table "ai2tabella" and then, in the top menu on the "Export" button.
It will be offered the SQL format that generally works well.

Rarely, for compatibility problems between different versions of phpMyAdmin installed on different servers, you must to use one of the other formats.
Only the user can determine which is the most suitable to the transfer format.
In any case, normally, has always been found that the suffix has permission to do so.

Once you make the choice of format, click on "Esegui".
The table will be "unloaded" on the PC in use in the predetermined position by the browser.

Load tables on the remote database

Load tables on the remote database

To load the table "ai2tabella" in the database on the Internet need to access phpMyAdmin on the remote server.

Aruba the address for access is http://mysql.aruba.it where you are asked to enter username and password provided by the operator.

For one.com access is from the control panel at https://login.one.com/cp/
Once inside, the phpMyAdmin functions the same way.

To the left is the list of databases, one in the case of one.com and 5 if the manager is Aruba.

In the case of Aruba must choose one by double-clicking on it.
The name of this database is to be included in the "ai2-connessionedb.php", which contains the parameters for the database connection.
(In $database = "appinventor2"; replace appinventor2 as sfornito by the provider).

Then click on the "Import" button, in the middle of the page will appear with the tools to do so.
You must select the import format, necessarily the same as that used in the export, then clicking the "Choose File" button, you can browse on the PC in use by selecting the previously exported file by then click on "Open"

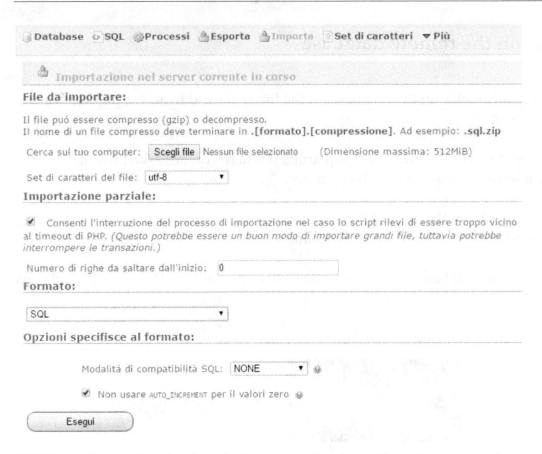

Will begin immediately after the import and at its end, at the top, on the same page, a message appears on the outcome of import.
If it is positive, the process is terminated; otherwise changing the type of format to repeat the export from the local database, then try to import again on the remote server

Prepare the page to connect to the database

The page "ai2-connessionedb.php" contains the parameters for the database connection. These are:
if ($ _SERVER ['SERVER_NAME'] == 'localhost') {
$ Hostname = "localhost";
$ Username = "root";
$ Password = "";
$ Database = "appinventor2";
}
else {
$ Hostname = "**11222333444**";
$ Username = "**Sql555555**";
$ Password = "**b77rd8888e**";
$ Database = "**Sql999999_5**";
}

Data in bold will be replaced with those provided by Aruba or another provider with whom you subscribe.

Done this page "ai2-connessionedb.php" to be saved.

Note that the database name is "**Sql999999_5**", this means that it is the database of Aruba number 5, if it were a real name, others would "**Sql999999_1**", "**Sql999999_2**", "**Sql999999_3**", "**Sql999999_4**"

Upload PHP pages to the web

Immediately after the purchase, the web space is ready, just need to reach to upload the php pages.

The methods used are varied including FileZilla, a free FTP in which once included the credentials supplied by the provider will show two windows on one local and one remote. Just drag and drop php pages from your PC on the remote window and you're done. Generally providers also have a File Manager utility that allows you to upload files from your PC in your web space.

In addition, with this utility you can create new folders, delete files and so on.

The providers also provide an utiliy -usually- called "File Manager"

After entering their credentials on the provider's website, from the Control Panel that has been assigned to the domain you log on to the "File Manager".

Even from here you can do the normal page load operations, create new folders, delete files and so on.

Folders available

The php pages may be loaded anywhere on the server, provided that all in the same folder, but should change the path on pages App.

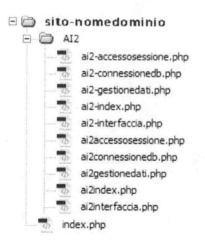

This path will be set in the App App_Web_PHP_MySQL.

The words domain name stands for the name of the selected domain.

The following diagram shows the layout of the php pages on any web space.

All in folder AI2

The index.php page is placed in the root folder of the web space, commonly known as "root" (tree of folders).

So once you had access to the "File Manager" to create a folder named "AI2".

To do it, write "AI2" in control Create Folder and click the icon next.

Double-click on the name of the "AI2" folder, opening it.

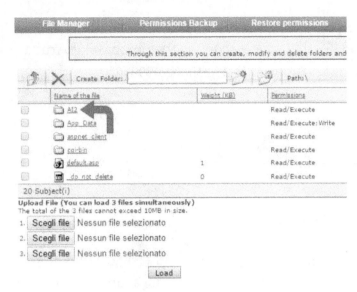

With the buttons below to select the your PC files:
ai2-accessosessione.php,
ai2-connessionedb.php,
ai2-gestionedati.php,
ai2-index.php,
ai2-interfaccia.php

ai2accessosessione.php,
ai2connessionedb.php,
ai2gestionedati.php,
ai2index.php,
ai2interfaccia.php

then click to upload the files.

Test pages and database on the Internet

Once sure that the php pages are all in the same "AI2" folder, the URL to the php pages will be:
http://nomedominio.ext/AI2/ai2-index.php, for access
http://nomedominio.ext/AI2/ ai2-interfaccia.php, App_Web_PHP_MySQL interface and the latest version of php
http://nomedominio.ext/AI2/ai2index.php, for access
http://nomedominio.ext/AI2/ ai2interfaccia.php, App_Web_PHP_MySQL interface and in a similar way for the other php pages loaded on the server.

Test access to the database and php version

Into your browser's address bar, type:
http://www.nomedominio.ext/AI2/ai2-connessionedb.php

Possible results:

- White page: the connection has been duly effected.
- White page with the string:
  Deprecated: mysql_pconnect (): The mysql extension is deprecated and will be removed in the future: use mysqli or PDO instead in D: \ inetpub \ webs \ domainname \ AI2 \ ai2-connessionedb.php online xy
  The connection has been regularly and php version is the latest.
  Use the 5 pages that does NOT contain the dash -

of possible error messages

Warning: mysql_pconnect (): No connection could be made Because the target machine actively refused it. in D: \ inetpub \ webs \ domainname \ AI2 \ ai2-connessionedb.php online xy

Fatal error: No connection could be made Because the target machine actively refused it. in D: \ inetpub \ webs \ domainname \ AI2 \ ai2-connessionedb.php online xy
There is probably an error in the data assigned to a variable:

$hostname, $username, $password, $database, controllare che i valori siano esatti.
To further check remove the characters / * and * / the underlying code that is in the login page and then save it and reload it in Intenet.

```php
<?php
/*
$query = "Select ai2tabella.id, ai2tabella.nome, ai2tabella.note, ai2tabella.data From
ai2tabella ";
$result = mysql_query($query) or die ("Quesry failed; " .mysql_error());
while ($row = mysql_fetch_array($result))
{echo "<br>".$row['id'], " - " , $row['nome'], " - " , $row['note'], " - " , $row['data'];}
*/
?>
```

By typing the URL http://www.nomedominio.ext/AI2/ai2-db.php access all records will appear.

In the test examples of these pages are used pages containing - (dash) but if the php version is more recent use of pages whose name is not - (hyphen).

Testing on Internet the ai2-interfaccia.php interface

Into your browser's address bar, type:
http: //www.nomedominio.ext/ AI2/ai2-interfaccia.php

The monitor should see a blank page.
If the message: Quesry failed; Table 'Sql888888_5.ai2tabella' does not exist,
the table was not found in the database
(Sql888888_5 replaces database name supplied by the provider).

To do further tests to change the default value to the variables
$IO = isset($_GET['IO']) ? $_GET['IO'] : 0;
Input Output 1 = selection / filtering 2 = returns the record id
Is
$id = isset($_GET['id']) ? $_GET['id'] : 0;
id of the requested record.
save, reload and launch the page

If $IO = 1 , all the records will appear if $IO = 2 the contents of the record with id = $ id

If the code on this page has the problems ai2-gestionedati.php page remains active with the danger of being used by fraudsters

Test the Internet-the ai2 index.php page

Into your browser's address bar, type:
http: //www.nomedominio.ext / AI2/ai2-index.php

Page will appear for a username and password.
wrong place them and press "Login", the page will be tested and recharged
"Ai2-index.php" listening for username and password entry.
Exact putting them and then pressing "Enter" will load the ai2-gestionedati.php page.

Username and Password are read line of code:
$ Username == "MiaUsername" and $ password = "MyPassword"
Replace MiaUsername and MiaPassword with others, save and reload the page on the Internet.

App_Web_PHP_MySQL

Having prepared the part php/MySQL, loaded on Internet servers, tested and ready, the next step is to assemble the app to communicate with table "ai2tabella" the remote database.

"App_Web_PHP_MySQL" is meant to show how to work with App for Android, through a php interface to a MySQL database is not accessible by ODBC driver.
The interface page "ai2-interfaccia.php".
For comprehensive guides on the App Inventor, also in Italian, see the official site of the MIT (Massachusetts Institute of Technology) at this address:
http://appinventor.mit.edu/explore/books.html

ODBC (Open DataBase Connectivity)

For large lines, it is a driver that uses the standard APIs allowing the connection from the client to the database. The API is independent of operating systems, programming languages and database systems.
The first version, such as DLLs, was developed on Windows, they followed for UNIX, OS/2 and Macintosh.

Remote data and management difficulties with App Inventor

With App Inventor (March 2016) the management of remote data can be made with various components, among them:

- TinyWebDB: It communicates with a Web service to store and retrieve information and make it available for other applications.
  Saving is necessarily in the form of pairs Tag / Value.
  Tag is the name that identifies the data and value the true value itself.
  With a practical example it is as if we put all data (contact, sentence etc.) In a bag (Value) and on each bag label (Tag) to locate and use.
  There are free web space that can be used to test applications with TinyWebDB but after testing the application requires the creation of its own service.

- FusiontablesControl: With this component you can store and share data in tabular format. Used for creation, selection, modification and deletion of data in tabular format, stored on Google Fusion Tables.
  https://developers.google.com/fusiontables/docs/v1/getting_started
  The systems using Fusion Tables applications require authentication for access to Google's servers and only work in this space.
  L 'authentication can be:

- o Key API for developers, allowing any manipulation of tables and data.
- o Account Service E-mail address, only for querying data.

Although excellent components in their operation, TinyWebDB is impractical to handle large amounts of data, while FusiontablesControl forces and use the Google servers.

Two other components of App Inventor allow access to web pages, they are WebViewer and Web

- WebViewer: Component to display Web pages.
  The URLs of the pages can be specified in the designer or editor of Blocks with GoToUrl method.
  In the Web Viewer window, you can surf the internet on as a normal browser.
  The URL can be inserted query-string to communicate with the code contained in the URL target page.
  With this component you can then issue commands and send the text to a specially written web page that can interact with a database.
- Web: Allows you to manage data through HTTP GET or HTTP POST.
  These methods allow you to query the web server issue commands, send text and receive data back.
  This data can be immediately accessible or processed by their own applications, the popular device pages or share them with the outside world.

Open App Inventor at http://appinventor.mit.edu/explore/
and click on "Create apps!".
Probably it will open the page "MIT App Inventor Beta 2" ready to assemble the App, alternatively may open a page where you are prompted for logon credentials.

App_Web_PHP_MySQL, how it works

The application interacts, through an interface, with the table "ai2tabella" of a database located on a server Intenet.
The database name can vary because often the provider establishes their name.
Examples are on Aruba servers but generalizable to other providers.
For App Inventor app "App_Web_PHP_MySQL" 2, the main componeti are three.

- **WebViewer** interfaces with "ai2-interfaccia.php" and issues commands to:
  Order any field of the table, in ascending and descending order
  Filter the data of a field of your choice, even the same order.
  The returned records will be visible on the device display.
- **Web** gives commands to "ai2-interfaccia.php" for:
  Import records from MySQL database to the Android device.
  The imported records will be visible on the display and ready for sharing.
- **Sharing** Component AI2 which allows file sharing and / or messages:
  By starting the component will display a list of installed applications on the device among those able to manage the information retrieved from the Web component.
  By choosing one of these applications, the sharing can take place eg. by electronic mail, social network, SMS, and so on.

The opening of the App choice for sharing, it already contains the data from the Web component and then ready to be used.
In App Inventor there are many methods to force the sharing in a certain way only for sending SMS, only for e-mail and so on.
Choosing Sharing has preferred to choose the user the sharing method you prefer, without forcing it may also produce errors by searching the App not installed on the device.

Designer page and components

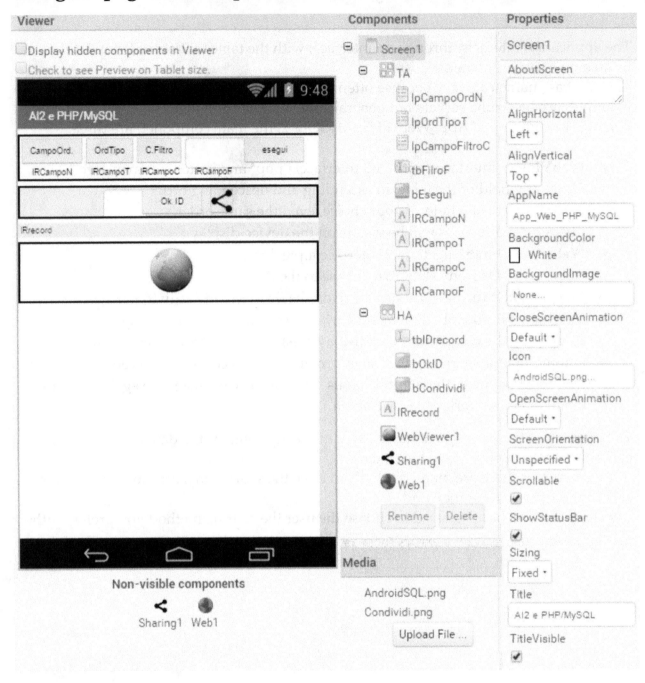

The last column represents the Screen1 properties.
For the properties of the other components see the next table.

Components, properties and functions

Components	Group	Name	Property
Screen1	AppName=App_Web_PHP_MySQL, Title= AI2 e PHP/MySQL		
Table.Arr.	Layout	TA	2 righe, 5 colonne, Alt. automatic, Larg. 100%
Container choice components, indexing, filtering on the fields, in line 2, label containing choices			
ListPicker	User Int.	lpCampoOrdN	FonSize=10, Alt. e Larg. automatic
Select the field on which will be done sorting records			
ListPicker	User Int.	lpOrdTipoT	FonSize=10, ElementsFromString=a-z,z-a Alt. e Larg. automatic
Select the type of sorting to be done on the chosen field with lpOrdTipoT (a-z, z-a)			
ListPicker	User Int.	lpCanpoFiltroC	FonSize=10, Alt. e Larg. automatic
Seleziona il campo che deve essere filtrato - Select the field that is to be filtered			
TextBox	User Int.	tbFilroF	FonSize=10, Hint=filtro Alt. automatic, Larg. 60pixel
Testo/filtro nella selezione dei record in ai2-interfaccia.php Text / filter in the record selection in ai2-interfaccia.php			
Button	User Int.	bEsegui	Name=esegui FonSize=10, Alt. automatic, Larg. 20%
Execute button bEsegui sends the interface commands ai2-interfaccia.php			
Label	User Int.	lRCampoN	FonSize=10, lRCampoN,Alt. e Larg. automatic
Will contain this choice with ListPicker lpCampoOrdN			
Label	User Int.	lRCampoT	FonSize=10, lRCampoT,Alt. automatic, Larg. 100%
Type of order chosen by lpOrdTipoT (a-z or z-a)			
Label	User Int.	lRCampoC	FonSize=10, lRCampoC Alt. e Larg. automatic
Will contain this choice with ListPicker lpCampoFiltroC			
Label	User Int.	lRCampoF	FonSize=12, lRCampoF,Alt. e Larg. automatic
Will contain the previously typed text in tbFilroF (the filter)			
Horizz.Arr.	Layout	HA	Alt. automatic, Fill parent
Container recovery comments and data sharing			
TextBox	User Int.	tbIDrecord	NumbersOnly=selezionato,FonSize=10, Hint=ID, Alt. automatic, Larg. 10%
D of the record to be retrieved			
Button	User Int.	bOkID	FonSize=10, Alt. automatic, Larg. 20%, il file Condividi.png da l'immagine al pulsante
Confirmation button for the ID to be recovered			
Button	User Int.	bCondividi	FonSize=10,Image=Condividi.png,Alt. e Larg.automatic
Lancia la condivisione del record con l'ID recuperato-Launches of the record shared with the retrieved ID			
Label	User Int.	lRrecord	FonSize=10,BackgroundColor=Yellow,Alt.automatic, Larg.100%
Will contain the contents of the records retrieved and ready for sharing			
WebViewier	User Int.	WebViewer1	Follow Links(Segui collegamenti)=abilitato Alt. automatic, Larg. automatic PromptforPermission=abilitato Visible=abilitato
Sharing	Social	Sharing1	Componente non visibile
Web	Connettivity	Web1	Componente non visibile
Retrieves data from ai2-interfaccia.php and places them in lRrecord			

Assign behaviors to components

link:
global variable "link" is declared, to which, with a text block is assigned as the value of the Internet interface address "ai2-interfaccia.php"
If when starting the App appears the message:
"Warning: mysql_pconnect (): No connection could be made Because the target machine actively refused it. in D: \ inetpub \ webs \ domainname \ AI2 \ ai2-connessionedb.php online xy "
the PHP version is outdated, replace the URL with the printed block below.
and in your application:
http: //www.VostroDominio/AI2/ai2interfaccia.php

initialize global ListaCampi to:
Global variable "ListaCampi" is declared.
The list will contain the names of the entries in ListPicker

lpCampoOrdN (CampoOrd.)
lpCanpoFiltroC (CanpoFiltro).

The voices of ListPicker are the same names of the camps run by the interface "Ai2-interfaccia.php".
The field names, for 2 ListiPicker, could also be declared in Designer picture in their ElementsFromString panes.
The choice to do so in the Blocks page is determined by the fact that the content of the two ListiPicker is identical.
This method avoids repeat 2 times the writing on the Designer tab,
It facilitates a possible modification of the list,
while decreasing the likelihood of errors.

When Screen1.Inizialize :

At the start is initialized Screen1 and populated the variable "ListaCampi" with the names of the camps run by the interface "ai2-interfaccia.php" for the table "ai2tabella" database.
The names of the fields in text blocks, are id, none, note, date.

Immediately after the lists are assigned to ListPicker
lpCampoOrdN -Campo on which to sort
lpCampoFiltroC - field on which to apply the filter
Finally the ValoriDiStart and NascondeImportazioneCondivisione procedures are invoked

to ValoriDiStart:
Procedure invoked after the initialization of Screen1, assigns the label that appears on the display defaults. With these values, in the case of a click on the button will perform the records will be sorted on the name field in the direction of a-z, and showing all records because the interface to the line that receives the command
$F = isset($_GET['F']) ? $_GET['F'] : "%";
the% character, acquired by default which means all records.

to NascondeImportazioneCondivisione:
Procedure invoked at the end of initialization and Screen1
by bEsegui block (to click on this button).
They are hidden:

lRecord: Label which must contain the records imported from the server to the device
bCondividi: Button for the share of imported records from the server to the device

it is emptied
tblDrecord: container of the record id to import
if-Reset, because there are none at startup
in the case of clicking on the button bEsegui because you prepare for new data.

Use of ListPicker

Similar to the Button component, at the click of ListPicker are displayed to the user a list of items from which to choose while remaining on hold.
When the user has chosen, the interface of ListPicker returns to its previous state.
In the case of this event App AfterPicking (after selected) is considered and taken Selection which corresponds to the ordinal number of the elements.
The same provision is in the interface in php receive the ordinal number of the field on which to operate with the important difference that:
ListPicke in the origin is 1 while in the interface fields is zero.
Sending data to the interface with the bEsegui button, the value 1 is subtracted from the result of ListPicker

When lpCampoOrdM AfterPicking:
ListiPicker that allows you to choose the field that will run the system.
To click on it appears the list of fields "ListaCampi"
identical to table fields "ai2tabella" database.
The user will have to click on one of them and
the result will be stored in the label lRCampoN.
It is a numeric value correspondent to the order of entries.
Value of the first item is equal to 1

When lpOrdTipoT AfterPicking:
ListiPicker that lets you choose the sort order between "a-z" and "z-a".
The content of this ListPicker is declared in the Designer page,
ElementsFromString pane.

Click on it to appear the rumors "a-z" and z-a.
The user will have to click on one of them and
the result will be stored in the label lRCampoT.
It is a numeric value correspondent to the order of entries.
Value of the first item is equal to 1

When lpCampoFiltroC AfterPicking:

ListPicker that lets you choose the field on which the filter will be applied.
To click on it appears the list of fields "ListaCampi"
identical to table fields "ai2tabella" database.
The user will have to click on one of them and
the result will be stored in the label lRCampoC.
It is a numeric value correspondent to the order of entries.
Value of the first item is equal to 1

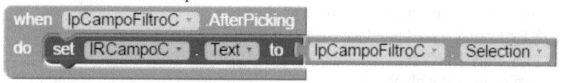

Select and filter records

when bEsegui click: Button that connects the WebViewer component interface "Ai2-interfaccia.php" passing values with the query-string method .

- Call tbFiltroF.HideKeyboard: Hides the virtual keyboard..
- set lRCampoF.Text to tbFiltro.Text: It fits into the label lRCampoF typed text into the tbFiltro component.
- set tbFiltro.Text to " ": Empty the filter component
- WebViewer1.GotoUrl : loads the page to the given URL
  It follows the block to join the text where they are "mounted" URL and querystring
    o get global link: URL interface "ai2-interfaccia.php"
    o ? : code that determines the opening of the query-string
    o N= :variable read interface with $N=isset($_GET['N']) ? $_GET['N'] : 1;
    o lpCampoOrdN.SelectionIndex-1: Field on which it will be done sorting. value passed with N -1 because the values returned by ListPicker start at 1 while the first field in the interface is the zero field.
    o & :identification new value to pass.
    o T = : variable read interface with $T = isset($_GET['T']) ? $_GET['T'] : 0;
    o lpCampoTipoN.SelectionIndex – 1: Sort Type "a-z" or "z-a" value passed with N -1 because the values returned by ListPicker start at 1 while in the interface the first value is zero.
    o & : identification new value to pass
    o C = : variable read interface with$C = isset($_GET['C']) ? $_GET['C'] : 2;
    o lpCampoTipoC.SelectionIndex – 1:Field on which the filter will be applied value passed with N -1 because the values returned by ListPicker start at 1 while the first field in the interface is the zero field.
    o & : identification new value to pass
    o F = : variable read interface with$F=isset($_GET['F']) ? $_GET['F'] : "%"; The % character, hired to default, means "all records"
    o lRCampoF.Text: : value passed with F call (already typed on TV Filtro.Text)
    o & : identification new value to pass
    o IO = 1: variable read interface with $IO = isset($_GET['IO']) ? $_GET['IO'] : 0; value 1 = selection / filtering
- NascondeImportazioneCondivisione: Hides Import Sharing: Hides unnecessary components at this stage.

When these blocks are run, the page "ai2-interfaccia.php" is running the query on ai2tabella table with the parameters received in the query-string.
The returned records are displayed on the display device.

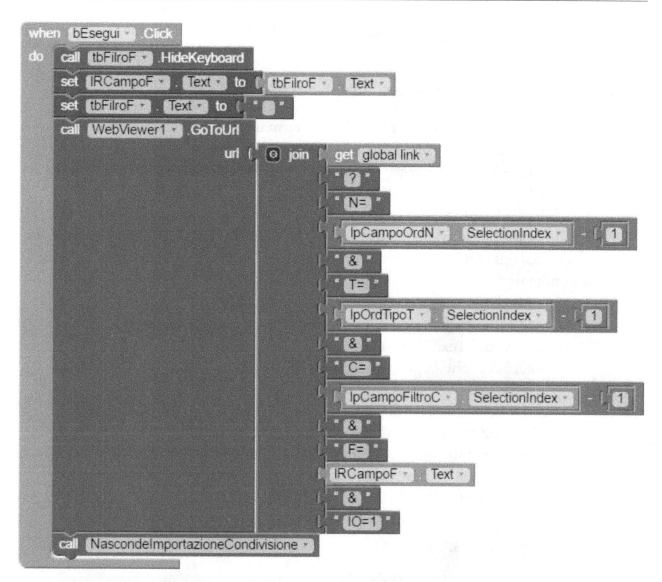

An example of the result of the execution of preceding block.
Having set:

- Sort field (CampoOrd.) = Name
- Order Type (OrdTipo) = z-a
- Filter field (C.Filtro) = date
- Filter = 2015

and clicked on the button Run,
for test records entered in the database, the result is to the left.
In fact, the record with id = 1 and id = 8
have been created or modified in 2015 as
you can read in the date field.

Import records into the device

When bOkID.click
Click to import the contents of the record with the index field value id

- Call tblDrecord.HideKeyboard: Hides the virtual keyboard.
- if not is number? idlDrecord.Text : if it is not a number
  then in September Idle record.Text to 0: 0 enter into component idlDrecord.Text
  null occurs without pressing this button values in idlDrecord.Text
- Set Web1.URL to: loads the page to the given URL
  It follows the block to join the text where they are "mounted" URL and querystring
- Get global link: Internet address of the interface that received the record id, return
  the contents of the record with that 'id.
- ? : code that determines the opening of the query-string
- Id= variable that contains the id of the record to be imported
  - tbIDrecord.Text: Value contained in the TextBox tbIDrecord sent to ai2-
    interfaccia.php page in querystring
    On the "ai2-interfaccia.php" code
    $id = isset($_GET['id']) ? $_GET['id'] : 0;
    You receive the id number of the requested record.
- & : identificator of the new value to process
  IO = 2: identification of new value starts to pass $IO = 2: variable read interface
  with $IO = isset($_GET['IO']) ? $_GET['IO'] : 0;
  value = 2 Returns the contents of the requested record in the block GotText

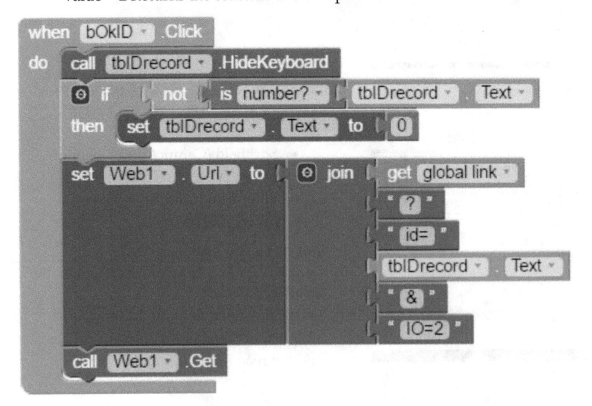

On the "interfaccia.php" after reading the query-string is launched a query on the id field (which has unique content) of the table.

If the query returns the records, the content of it is copied to the $ variable text, or in the variable $ text is inserted: "The record $ id does not exist."

Finally, with echo $ text is sent to the device

When Web1.Got:text
returns the contents of the record for for id required.

- set lRrecord.text to trim
    - trim: remove any spaces at the beginning and end of the string received
        - get responseContent: the value is returned in response Content, then inserted in the Label lRrecord

          trim remove any spaces at the beginning and end of string
- set lRrecord.Visible to true: It makes visible the label that contains the contents of the returned records (the one with the yellow background)
- set bCondividi.Visible to true: it makes visible the button for record sharing

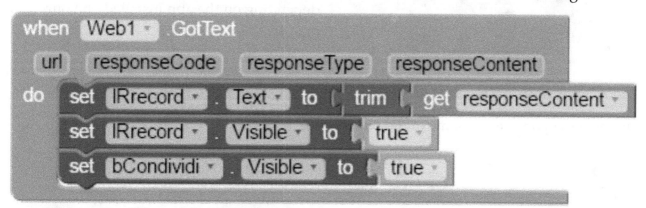

As result of execution of the preceding block.

Inserting 8 in the TextBox "tbIDrecord" and pressing the Button "Ok ID" has been requested the record with id = 8 from the remote database.

The contents of the record with id = 8 has been imported and placed in the Label "lRrecord"
(On yellow background).

The button for records sharing has appeared.

Share the content of the imported records

At this point, the records can be shared with the rest of the world by clicking on the button that has bCondividi on whether the symbol: <

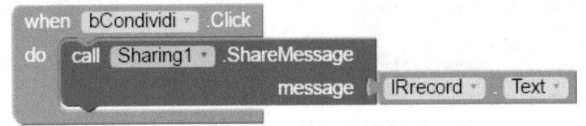

Clicking on the button opens a window similar to:

The contents of the window changes depending on the app installed on your device.

Below how you present some of the possibilities

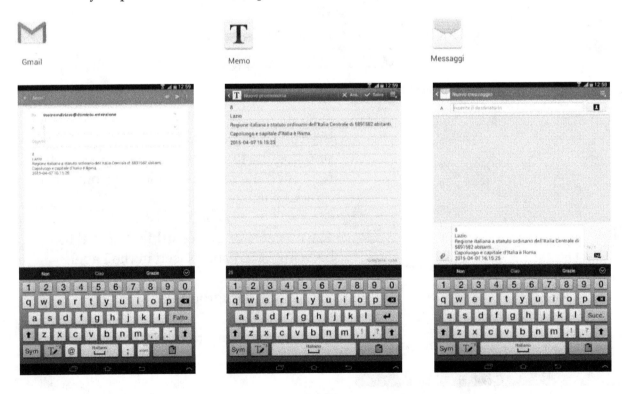

The official website for App Inventor project http://appinventor.mit.edu/explore/

Terms and conditions for use of the software provided.
The Hague / APK files have been successfully tested on Android devices.
For large quantity and diversity of Android devices available on the market it has been impossible to test the examples on each of them.
For this reason it can not be guaranteed that all the examples work on every device.
THE SOFTWARE IS PROVIDED "AS IS", WITHOUT WARRANTY OF ANY KIND, EXPRESS OR IMPLIED, INCLUDING, BUT NOT LIMITED TO, IMPLIED WARRANTIES OF MERCHANTABILITY, 'FITNESS' FOR A PARTICULAR PURPOSE AND NON-INFRINGEMENT. IN NO EVENT SHALL THE AUTHORS OR COPYRIGHT HOLDERS BE LIABLE FOR ANY CLAIM, DAMAGES OR OTHER LIABILITY, WHETHER IN AN ACTION OF CONTRACT, TORT OR OTHERWISE, ARISING FROM, OR IN CONNECTION WITH THE SOFTWARE OR THE USE OR OTHER DEALINGS WITH THE SOFTWARE.

address:
http://www.taccetti.net/App_Web_PHP_MySQL/

They are downloadable database table, php pages and App_Web_PHP_MySQL
here will also be available for updating and / or corrections.
For communications use the form:
http://www.app-inventor.it/Contatti/Contatti.php

www.ingramcontent.com/pod-product-compliance
Lightning Source LLC
Chambersburg PA
CBHW060459060326
40689CB00020B/4589